Tick Tock:
It's Time to Listen

A collection of poetry
by
Lauren Smith

Tick Tock: It's Time to Listen
By Lauren Smith

© 2019 Lauren Smith
ISBN: 9781912092963

First published in 2019 by Arkbound Ltd (Publishers)
Illustrated by Sam Potter

Arkbound is a social enterprise that aims to promote social inclusion, community development and artistic talent. It sponsors publications by disadvantaged authors and covers issues that engage wider social concerns. Arkbound fully embraces sustainability and environmental protection. It endeavours to use material that is renewable, recyclable or sourced from sustainable forest.

Arkbound
Backfields House
Upper York Street
Bristol BS2 8QJ
England

www.arkbound.com

Tick Tock:
It's Time to Listen

Foreword

I have been aware of Lauren's fantastic work in raising awareness of autism for a few years now. It is a pleasure to read this collection of her poems.

I am also a female with an Autism Spectrum Disorder ('ASD'), and I can strongly relate to many of the thoughts and feelings Lauren writes about in her poetry. ASD causes a person to have difficulties communicating, but some people like Lauren have found other, brilliant ways to communicate.

I really like the hope that shines through in some of these poems. ASD is most often depicted in a negative light in the sense that there tends to be a focus on the struggles. Lauren has very nicely turned this around by; for example, highlighting many of the good experiences she has had and how other people have successfully helped her. She talks about the inspiring teachers who fit their method of teaching to her, rather than try to fit her to their method of teaching. In 'No-One Judge, Judge No-One' she describes a school that provided a very enjoyable learning experience.

Some of the poems are sad. The difficulties Lauren writes about resonate to many people on the autistic spectrum. I have no doubt that many people will be able to relate to these words and that they will help make the experience of living with an ASD a bit less of a lonely place. Just to know that somebody else feels the same way is very comforting.

I very much enjoyed reading Lauren's poetry. She has a way with words. And the fact that ASD by definition entails difficulties communicating makes these poems extra special.

Alis Rowe
Founder of The Curly Hair Project

Introduction

Autism is a neurological condition which affects everyone differently. There is currently a large amount of stigma attached to what is considered to be a 'disabling condition. I have written a series of poems to reflect upon my experiences of living with High Functioning Autism. Through my poetry, I aim to dispel the myths and encourage society to realise how liberating, inspiring and intriguing autism can be. A combination of negativity and hopeful messages are portrayed in the poems to represent how my emotions contrast on a daily basis.

I'm Sorry

This poem provides a glimpse of how I feel living with High Functioning Autism. This poem was written to reflect the intense feelings I had for one of my friends at school. I felt extremely attached to my friend yet struggled immensely to connect with her. My heightened anxiety and low self-esteem prevented me from communicating my feelings to her. This poem aims to channel my perception of the world into an understandable format so that my friend can relate to me and support me.

I'm sorry I don't always smile,
I really don't want to run a mile.

I'm sorry I don't seem to understand you,
I come from a different planet, which happens to be blue.

I'm sorry I don't always speak,
The way I initiate conversation makes me look weak.

I'm sorry you need to wait for me to respond,
It may seem, to you, like I want to abscond.

I'm sorry I interpret things in a different way,
I really do try my best every day.

I'm sorry I act a fool in crowds,
Everyone is just so overwhelming and loud.

I'm sorry if I come across as rude,
But I think it's better than me being nude.

I'm sorry if I appear lame,
But one day, I promise you, I'll have my claim to fame.

I'm sorry my challenges and struggles seem stupid,
That's probably why I haven't found cupid.

I'm sorry I sometimes misread the signs,
I can't understand why you don't want to be mine.

I'm sorry I don't show my emotions,
It's difficult for me to show my devotion.

I'm sorry I don't tell you how I feel,
Sometimes, my life just seems too unreal.

I'm sorry I never tell you how much I care,
My way of showing you I care is by thinking about what I wear.

I'm sorry my aspirations seem unachievable,
Yours seem much more believable.

I'm sorry I tend to ignore you,
But, deep down, I'm noticing every way to woo you.

I'm sorry I can't express how much you mean to me,
Love is as hard to explain as it is to see.

I'm sorry I'm not as good as you'd no doubt like me to be,
But I need you to know that you mean the world to me.

I'm sorry I'm soon going to vanish,
But proving 'I love you' is one thing I have accomplished.

I'm Sorry

Bullies

This poem is based on three girls that I considered to be my friends, however they turned against me and were quite spiteful. This poem awarded me with a certificate of being an 'Anti-Bullying Champion' and represents bullying on a general level. It's not particularly representative of the bullying I experienced, however the emotions I recall and the importance of standing up for yourself resonate.

I'm stuck in a dark hole,
I feel trapped,
There's no way out, no way forward,
It's the bullies, yes that's right: the bullies.

They push me, punch me and purposely swear,
They even dare to pull my hair.

My thoughts are broken; torn apart,
I cry alone at night – every night – every single night,
"Nobody cares, you're worthless," they call
In real life and in the voices in my head.

I yearn to run away; to escape,
To wander and wonder
What life would be like if I was more confident and sociable.

I came to the conclusion,
With all the thought intrusion,
Sending me into an isolating world of delusion:
I had to stand up to the bullies.

I'd lasted too long through agonizing pain,
My constant tears represented in the pouring rain.
I had to show the bullies what I was made of;
I am strong-minded, beautiful and compassionate,
Not deserving of the torment, isolation and heartbreak.

"Make a noise about bullying," called out a friend of mine,
"Make your voice heard," she proclaimed,
"Stand up for what is right, not wrong,
And together we can stop bullying!"

Lonely

A poem to represent how I felt after being picked on by the three girls who I thought were my friends; I felt isolated and worthless. I struggle to make new friends at the best of times, let alone when my confidence has been shattered.

They call me 'weird', 'rude' and 'odd',
So off I go on my lonely tod,
They patronise and criticise me,
Say "everyone loves me, but everyone hates you, you see."

They chat about me rather than to me and pull
faces in my direction,
Causing provoked awkwardness and tension,
They snigger constantly behind my back,
Say "you should run away and leave as soon as
you've packed your lonely sack."

They make me feel lonely,
Sour-hearted like guacamole,
I feel like I'm not good enough:
Pathetic, queasy, rough.

It doesn't matter if they don't physically hurt me,
They are emotionally killing me!
Words hurt more than anyone can ever realise,
At my darkest moments, my future is impossible to visualise.

Thing is, I'm reserved and bashful as it is,
I know this; I don't need to look at a quiz,
I am an inspirational, unique person,
The bullying and my loneliness have caused a
thought aversion.

Friendship

A poem I've written to compare a fake friend to a true friend (a concept I struggled to understand when I was at school). This poem is based on the three girls who I considered to be my friends, but who turned against me and also turned others away from me. I've used the theme park as an imaginative metaphor for a fake friend. At the end of each stanza, I aim to briefly describe what a true friend is. True friends accept you for who you are, fake friends aren't worth your time or energy.

Friendship bends,
Goes round corners,
Swirls round and round
And rides up and down.

Friendship whizzes,
Kisses and misses,
But does not diss.

Sat on a rollercoaster, front seat screaming,
The turbulence of the ride makes you realise you can't hide.
Friends are there to listen, care and guide,
Friendship is the reason we survive through tough times.

Sitting in dazzling teacups,
Your friendship gradually fading to a blur,
You feel dizzy and sick; you can't see your friend clearly.
Friends are supposed to wipe away tears before they arrive,
Pat you on the back and say "hey, well done,"
And shoo away any negative loonies.

The horror of the ghost train
Sharply swaying round corners,
Wanting to scare the living hell out of you.
Friends support you through frightening phases
And want you to feel comfortable.

Get out of the theme park immediately!

Don't ever go there again!

True friends will love you, even when you don't love yourself.

True friendship is like an orchestra –

Where all the instruments play softly to the same tune.

Love Is...

This short poem represents my perception of love: a complex and confusing topic. Often, people assume that people on the autism spectrum are incapable of finding love because of their social navigation difficulties, however I believe the complete opposite is true. We can all find love, we may just express our emotions differently.

Love is comforting,

Love is warm,

Love is confidence boosting,

Love is kind,

Love is enthusiastic,

Love is motivating,

Love is encouraging,

Love is life.

Love

This poem is based on how I imagine a relationship breakdown to feel – soul destroying. I based this poem on one of my friends that I had intense feelings for. When there was an option to leave mainstream education, I was incredibly apprehensive because I didn't know how I could accept leaving my friend behind.

Love tears deep into flesh,
No-one truly knows the intensities of the emotion,
until they have experienced it truly.

Love scorns, the minute it is born,
"Love hurts", an anonymous alert,
Love makes tears flow like the ocean,
Love puts feelings into motion.

Burning as hot as red can burn –
symbols of love yet symbols of fire,
Excruciating pain,
Soul destroying,
Physically hating, mentally still loving –
No-one can truly describe a relationship breakdown,
until they have been through the storm.

No purpose on Earth,
No reason for life,
My lover has vanished into thin air,
Now all that's left is silly old me, weeping with despair.

The anger, the guilt, the hate and the fear,
The jealousy, the confusion, the stupidity and the heartbreak,
Terrorises the already mental mind,
Makes you go insane,
And makes you feel like you've been hit by a train.

Long term relationships, in the minority,
Must compose of everything, yet nothing derogatory.
If you've loved the same person for 10 years or more,
Then the animation of your love must be defined and recognised in the toy store.

Different and Depressed to Strange and Smiling

This poem was written to describe the depressive thoughts that constantly exploded in my mind, as I struggled to cope with bullying and difficulties socialising. It represents how during the most difficult times, there was someone at school that did look out for me and wanted to connect with me. She tried endlessly to understand the complex wiring of my mind, however I was too anxious to respond. This poem aims to bring hope to people who are suffering with depression and anxiety, showing that, even though you may feel alone, there are people who care about you.

Fragmented, crumbling, jumbled,
Hiding in her shell, never wanting to appear again,
"I can't do this anymore," she mumbled,
Her list of friends didn't even make it to ten.

In the mirror, she stares at her puzzled self,
"I give up," she sobbed,
No happiness, definitely no wealth,
Of any love, friendship and voice, she felt she was robbed.

The dirt on her window distorts her reflected image,
Her vivid visions and her view,
Lights from the houses shone through the village,
The local competition for pretty models, she would be last in the queue.

The rain splashes loudly against her face,
Sat in a dark, lonely ditch, totally lost in thought,
She silently screams: "I'm just a waste,"
Cold, friendless, distraught.

In a dismal state of mind:
"Everyone hates me, I'm no good,"
She didn't realise she was one of a kind,
Her negative thoughts escalated, as much as they could.

Complacent, stubborn, egotistical,
She believed the bullies, "I deserve the torment,"
How could she ever feel mystical?
She had no outlet to help her vent!

Her differences were no longer embraced,
She had quickly spiralled into depression,
Nobody could save her; she was trapped and couldn't be traced,
Her snail-pace speed had led to mental aggression.

Her not-so-dysfunctional family at home awaits her presence,
Despaired, anxious, frantic,
But they were patient: "this is probably the norm in adolescence,"
For their daughter, they would swim the Atlantic...

As she wept alone, she noticed a light,
In hope she could be invisible, she sat tight,
But she soon heard footsteps approach,
All she wanted to do was get away via coach.

The girl called to her, ran and sat beside her,
She could see she was fragile, vulnerable and naïve,
She offered a hug and hoped she wouldn't deter,
The girl refused to leave.

Soon after, as the tears had dried, they recognised each other,
She spoke softly, showing sadness and shyness,
It was like a sister being reunited with her long-lost brother,
She was fatigued, her distortion of thoughts had caused
extreme tiredness.

An hour zoomed by,
So they safely got home,
Her school friend said: "I don't want you to cry,"
She said, "you'll never walk alone."

She couldn't care what her parents said,
The most important thing was she did have a friend,
Laid safely in bed,
She dreamed of how she would never, never again pretend.

Depression is isolating,
But there is always hope,
Your negativity can be violating,
But don't sit there thinking you're a mope!

Dedicated to You

This poem was written to send my appreciations to a support worker from an autism outreach team. She was absolutely amazing and truly understood me. Without her, I would've ended up having a nervous breakdown and wouldn't have been able to continue my education. As I was on a reduced timetable, she met me at school whenever I attended, which was two days a week. She helped me to find my smile again. However, due to circumstances when I left the school, she was unable to keep supporting me. The support was transferred to a new school with a smaller unit for students with medical needs.

You're fun-loving, enthusiastic and kind,
To some people, your love may be blind,
But I realise how your talents and passions shine through,
And respect and love you for all that you set out to do.

You work hard to achieve the best for everyone,
Ensuring that students with additional needs can
have good fun.

Striving to offer support and inspiration,
Aiming to desensitise students and free their aggravations.

Your main intention is to mention the interventions that
should be offered to students who struggle,
After all, it's down to you, as their heads are in a muddle.

You set a mission to replace any disgrace,
With a caring and cheerful face.

You have the world's greatest vision,
To encourage schools and services to provide thoughtful
provision.

Working with students with social and emotional
difficulties is a challenging and brave thing to do,

But in the end, it's worth it, as all the love and praise comes back to you.

You've tried so hard to guide, care and love,
And I want to send an angel to watch over you, from above.

Look after yourself and enjoy life,
You deserve every second of happiness and joy,
You are one of my best friends,
And you mean the world to me.

No One Judge, Judge No One

A poem written to represent the new school I was referred to, Voyage Learning Campus (VLC). Providing one-to-one support and an individualised programme, it was a safe haven and offered an enjoyable learning experience. I was encouraged to make friends with people from all different backgrounds, which widened my social network. This new school was my lifeline.

I know a place where no one will judge,
A safe haven, quiet and secure.
The quirks of the teachers, the cries of the children,
Yet no one will judge them.

I know a place where no one will judge,
The students, vulnerable and isolated.
They gradually manage to speak up,
Yet no one will judge them.

I know a place where no one will judge,
The kids dressed in rags and tear.
The parents have no money to spare,
Yet no one will judge them.

I know a place where no one will judge,
Hair dye, piercings, fake tattoos or fags.
Only to attempt to be like the crowd,
Yet no one will judge them.

I know a place where no-one will judge,
Overweight, underweight.
Apprehensive, impulsive,
Yet no one will judge them.

So, if people are happy for you to be you,
Why aren't you happy for them?
I know a place where no-one will judge,
Go there, teach, support, guide and love.
After all, you don't want to be judged!

Her Love

This poem was written to explore a 'crush' I had for a student at school. When I finally overcame my low self-esteem and approached him, I stumbled and made a mistake. I have realised that it's important to be yourself and it's acceptable to make mistakes. Despite my love for him, nothing blossomed. I just thought of it as another learning opportunity and confidence booster.

Sat in the corner was his pale face,
He was introverted and weak,
His history the girl was unable to trace,
She didn't know about the support he could seek.

From a distance, the girl watched,
While he played games on his phone,
The girl's thoughts were blotched,
It looked like he was happy alone.

She could hear the shouts of the kids next door,
'he shouldn't be on his own,' she thought,
Loud noises and crowds were two things that she did abhor,
The mission to communicate with him she didn't want to abort.

But, all of a sudden, a swear word and thud came from above,
The embarrassed girl rushed into the room next door,
All she could think about was her love,
She sat in silence and stared blankly at the floor.

Guilt and anxiety trickled down her cheeks,
Going through conversation over and over in her head,
Thinking about her love, but also counting down the weeks,
'I have autism', she thought. Enough said.

Overwhelmed in social situations,
Body language, she couldn't grasp,
Deep down, she wanted to impress and smile in front
of a standing ovation,
Conversation was the most difficult task.

Her frustrations and aggravations almost defined her,
Desperate for a day to put her differences aside,
To be in the shoes of her best friend she would prefer,
Her confused, controlling thoughts were constant and tied.

All of a sudden, the kids were called to class,
The girl looked up and dried her tears,
She stood silently and peered at her love, sat alone,
through the glass,
She smiled to herself, to try to rid the fear.

As she shyly approached him,
The girl's thoughts stumbled in panic,
Standing before him, she exclaimed: "Hi Tim!"
He must have thought she was manic,
He stopped his game and looked ahead, to see the girl,
She realised, as he looked puzzled, that 'Oh hell, that
wasn't his name.'
Maybe, she could've impressed him if she had done a
professional swirl.
She didn't want him to think she was lame,
At least she had gained his attention,
Their eyes locked and they stared at each other in amazement,
But, she figured, she should have some more social skills
interventions.
Regardless of this, the girl continued to look at him in
admiration.

Teachers

A poem to describe the inspiring teachers I had at my new school. As people often say, the importance of a good teacher cannot be emphasised enough. I felt confident in confiding in them, as they genuinely understood me and how autism affects me. This poem expresses how all that is needed is a positive attitude and creative approach. Meeting support needs isn't all determined by funding, or lack of, for that matter.

I never thought I could build a bond so strong,
Thoughtful, loving and kind.
Especially with people that I haven't known for long,
If I had the chance, this year I would rewind.

Intriguing, inspirational and influential,
Spreading positivity around the school.
You made me realise my potential,
Just by using thought and initiative, rather than specialist teacher tools.

Not only have you given me basic subject knowledge,
Teaching me chemistry, algebra and assonance.
You have also encouraged me to feel more enthusiastic about getting whisked away to college,
Slowly and surely, developing my confidence.

You were dedicated to supporting me,
Gently challenging me.
Encouraging me to be who I want to be,
Maximising my ability for the future, even though the 'confident' me was hard to see.

You understood and accepted me,
At the Voyage Learning Campus, I felt like I belonged.
You allowed me to express myself and be free,
Of all of you, I am very fond.

I don't want to lose a piece of my heart that I can't replace,
So even though I can't come back every day,
I've locked all the precious moments and photos in a secret case,
To reflect on the memories every day, to help wipe the tears away.

Teachers like you are hard to find,
Difficult to leave,
And impossible to forget,
That's why I want to say "I love you."

Thank You Teachers

This poem was written to give a heartfelt message of thanks to my teachers. My teachers were proactive in ensuring that all the students achieved their full potential. They expressed a caring and cheerful nature, which is thoroughly important when teaching students with autism. I was incredibly anxious about leaving this school and the support of the teachers, so they offered me a transition plan, whereby I had extra one-to-one lessons when the rest of the students had left school.

At VLC tuition,
The teachers create a mission,
To reach all of the students there,
Even when school's too much for them to bear.

The teachers encourage the quietest to interact,
And the loudest not to distract,
The anxious students learn to venture out of their cave,
And the 'difficult to handle' students are taught to behave.

The teachers never give up or fail to raise a smile,
The love and influence of each teacher goes more than a mile,
Their job is to teach, support and guide,
To ensure that each individual's knowledge can be applied.

To teach an anxious or challenging student is a hard and brave thing to do,
Their world you need to look out a different window to view,
For each student the teachers create a vision,
Despite the student's negative thoughts making a collision.

The teachers teach the students to recognise that their aggravations,
Could in fact inspire an aspiration,
Previous experiences could contribute to the student's future,
But in the end, it all comes down to whether they have a good tutor.

Prom Night

After building in confidence at the Voyage Learning Campus, I decided to go back to my old school for their prom night. I wanted to show how much strength I had gained. I was still anxious about the big social gathering though. This poem reflects my anxiety around approaching the girl I had intense feelings for. But, I had realised that I have friends and no matter what happens, they would always be by my side.

There's me, then there's her,
I'm bashful, she's beautiful,
I clam up and freeze, whilst she dances freely, laughing with her friends,
How will I feel confident enough to be like her on prom night?

I hope she smiles to me,
I hope she says hello,
I hope she invites me to her group,
But, of course, until prom night we won't know.

Endless thoughts circle round and round,
I'm trying not to panic,
But sometimes anxiety overrules and I frantically freeze,
All I can think of is what will happen on prom night.

'What should I do?' I ask myself,
'What will I do?'
I ask myself numerous what if's,
Trying to work out a plan for every situation on prom night.

What will I do on prom night
If it rains, if it pours?
If the buffet is disgusting?
If the music is so outdated?

But, more importantly, what I will do on prom night
if she doesn't speak?
Or even glance?
Or the other extreme, if everyone stares and glares?
If people mock me behind my back?

The main thing I want at prom is for her to be kind
and welcoming,
I want her to say "hi" and smile and capture the
moment on camera,
I hope she will be my friend,
Not just on prom night, but for the future.

I've thought and thought about prom night,
An important and memorable milestone,
I've tried so hard to think of a solution for every problem,
And a positive for every negative.

I've come to the decision that whatever happens,
I know people care about me,
And I will enjoy myself on prom night,
Celebrating saying goodbye to my school years.

I have friends,
Not everyone at prom knows the real me,
And I know not everyone will care on prom night,
But some people do!

That Girl

This poem reflects upon how much confidence I've gained since leaving mainstream secondary school. My achievements may seem insignificant, however, in my experience, they are milestones that should be celebrated.

That girl who hid in isolation in her English class, frozen with fear because she had to read her poetry in front of everyone,
Has now managed to conquer her fear and is proud to showcase her insightful and heart-warming poetry to share her perspective of the world.

That girl who sat in the lonely corner of the lunch hall eating her triangular cucumber sandwiches,
Now realises that it doesn't matter what shape the bread is and that it's more enjoyable to
share your sandwiches with someone.

That girl who was heartbroken at her friend's betrayal when she needed them most,
Now realises that true friends love you for who you are and people who can't accept you,
aren't worth it.

That girl who cried alone every night at the fact she couldn't speak to anyone,
Now has the confidence to attempt to initiate conversation.

That girl who was afraid to make any friends in case they broke her heart and left her,
Now realises that true friends won't leave her side and will support her during difficult times.

That girl who continuously crumbled under all of the social and academic pressure,
Threatening to have a nervous breakdown,

Now has coping strategies and is more capable of managing her anxieties.

That girl who was near to losing hope and giving up,
Is now a stronger person and is determined to succeed and make the most out of life.

That girl who was an emotional wreck, crying uncontrollably and trying endlessly to find an appropriate way to express and cope with her frustrations,
Is now able to look to her friends for love and support, and can unleash her mixed emotions,
Into writing and turn to her passions for motivation.

That girl who compared herself and her abilities to a more confident, more successful and prettier student in her class,
Now respects herself and has learnt to just be happy as she is, feeling proud of every single achievement she manages to make.

That girl who was ashamed and embarrassed to be herself in front of others for fear of getting mocked and defriended yet again,
Has now learnt to embrace her differences and stand out from the crowd.
She adds vibrancy to the world and no longer worries what other people think or say about her.

That girl who used to be weak and quiet,
Now has the guts to stand powerfully to get what she deserves!

My Friend

This is a poem to represent how confused and frustrated I was about the feelings I had for one of my friends, who was always there for me. This poem tells the story of the journey I went on with her. After developing the confidence to meet up with her outside of school, one of the bullies sent me a spiteful message online and my friend stuck up for me, getting herself into trouble. People spread rumours about the incident and upset my friend, which unfortunately led to the breakdown of our friendship. I was always curious as to what was said about me whilst at school.

I want you to know that, because of you,
I'm no longer blue.

You're so beautiful, supportive and kind,
I just wish you could understand my mind.

I wish I could speak,
To you, I must appear weak.

I'm desperate to express my emotion,
But it's hard for me to show my devotion.

It's a miracle that we went out together,
I was hoping we could go out forever.

It is strange how one person can ruin all we had,
But I want you to realise that I wasn't trying to make you mad.

The dark, depressing feelings you give me,
All I want is to sit down and make you a cup of tea.

Once, all you did was protect,
Now, all you do is reject.

I wish I had said hello first,
Maybe our friendship wouldn't have been cursed.

This is tearing me apart,
From you I never thought I'd depart.

You need to realise what you mean to me,
But I suppose it's hard for you to see.

I really want you to be my friend,
If you're upset, my shoulder I will always lend.

Simply the Best

This is a poem I wrote for my 'friend' when she got a new job. Due to the friendship breaking down, she was unaware that I wrote this, but I am hoping that this message will reach her one day.

Good luck – you'll be great,
Even if it's something you hate,
Give it a try,
And you'll soar after you learn to fly.

Try not to worry,
And not get in a tizz or a hurry,
Don't care if people judge you,
You are trying your best – you are new.

I don't know exactly what you're doing,
As different lives we are viewing,
But I know you'll be really good at everything you do,
I'll see you soon – hopefully chat – even if I have to be the last in the queue.

The message I want you to receive is,
You always have been, are and always will be, a whizz,
I care and want you to do well,
But as we all know, only time will tell.

I'm encouraging you through poetry,
Even though I know you wouldn't vote for me,
You're not like the rest,
You are simply the best.

Appreciated

A poem I've written that aims to reflect my friend's perception of me. As my friend had also struggled in the past, she truly understood my long trudge of a path. She was genuinely there for me and tried to support me in whatever she could, waiting aimlessly for my response.

I can see through the strain,
I can understand your pain,
For you, school is rain and more rain.

Your fear is clear to see,
I know you perceive situations differently to me,
Your education is full of animosity.

I appreciate it may take a while until you smile,
A few weeks until you speak,
And a year for you to hear that you're loved and accepted...
by me.

I'm not here to break your heart,
I don't want you to depart,
I'm here to be your friend and share my jam tarts.

I know you have awe-tism,
I will not allow your depressing thoughts to trap you in an
unwanted, unnoticed prison,
I will stand by you to help you battle your collisions.

Please don't be scared of me,
I'm here to set you free,
You can find your sunshine,
And feel appreciated and divine.

You will find light in your path,
You will learn to smile and laugh,
You will dream big and reach high like a giraffe,
But until then, I'll be with you, so your anxious, angry and
alienating thoughts don't break you in half.

In me, you should have faith,
For you'll then maybe see a glimpse; a trace,
Of my misunderstandings, confusions and isolations that I
lock into a saddened case,
That I don't show on my laughing, loveable face.

What Did You Do That For?

This poem is based on my feelings surrounding my friend blocking me on social media, after she got herself in trouble. I desperately wanted to connect with her, so I contacted her regularly (perhaps too often). I think it's fair to say that the majority of my friendships were, and still are, based on my terms.

I am angry, frustrated and confused by this situation,
It's full of misunderstandings and miscommunications,
Like most of my friendships are.

This friendship, though, I was led to believe was unique,
But, obviously I was wrong, it's just like all of the others:
Cold. Craved. Complicated.

After all we've been through, I can't understand why you've hit the block button,
How have I hurt you? What did you do that for?
Tell me please!

I don't trust that you will,
But I beg for you to accept my apologies,
Thought you were understanding, accepting and supportive.

You may think that I've moved on,
But, I still need to know why you've done it,
For acceptance? For a lesson? For you? For me?

Believe it or not, I still think of you,
The memories will never fade,
I hope you remember me in years to come.

I wonder how life's treating you,
Of course, I'll never know and I don't think you'll ever tell,
But deep down, I wish you all the best.

In years to come, I'll say hello to you,
Send my apologies once again,
And hope that you'll reply.

Just Like You

A poem I've written for my friends who soon turned into enemies. I suppose the majority of my peers could benefit from reading this too. This poem explores my personal wishes, which you will probably realise are extremely similar to those of neuro-typicals. I aim to reduce the barriers that society puts up for people with autism and encourage them to achieve their dreams.

I want to have a close friend,
I want to enjoy my studies at college,
I want to live independently in the future,
I want to achieve my ambition of attending university,
I want to fall in love and experience a romantic relationship,
I want to get a good job,
I want to be happy and successful,
Just like you!

I want my voice to be respected,
I want my ideas to be appreciated,
I want to experience the wonder of the world,
I want to explore natural beauty at its depths,
Just like you!

So, the next time you want to discriminate,
victimise or isolate a person with autism,
Please remember we are just like you,
Deep down – the same as everyone else,
We just act differently on the surface!

Just like you

Resilient

This poem offers a glimpse of the negativity I experienced whilst at mainstream secondary school. Reflecting on how one support lady from a specialist autism team (Vulnerable Learner's Service) practically changed my life, it shows the importance of hope and understanding.

You listen to your negative self-talk and intrusive comments from your 'fake friends';
you compare yourself to your so-called 'perfect best friend,'
You drag yourself down, deeper and deeper as the days go on; you're emotionally exhausted
from continually feeling like a failure.
You feel demoralised and alone; your thoughts are either invisible or considered as 'alien' by everyone else,
The way you are upsets you.
"Why can't I just fit in and make a friend?"; "Why am I too anxious to smile to people?"
Angry, guilty, pathetic sobs on your pillow every night; no-one hears you. You wonder how
long you have left to calm yourself down.

After what felt like a lifetime of feeling disheartened with who I am,
A support lady, who happened to believe in me, managed to inspire me to seek further support.
She said "you can do it; you're amazing."
She taught me to have faith in myself, to be proud of who I am and to start loving the beautiful and inspirational person I am.
The dark, dingy 'prison' of mainstream secondary had actually shown me what a strong young woman I am.
I may have struggled and I may continue to struggle,
But I am resilient. And I am proud to be myself.

Resilient

College

A poem I've written to capture my heightened anxieties surrounding taking the leap to college – a daunting prospect. After the immense stress of school, I was unsure of what future I would have at college and was apprehensive of the new beginning.

Battling anxiety, confusion and negativity,
Hoping to succeed academically and socially,
I try to see my future clearly and vividly,
Aiming not to burn out emotionally.

My thoughts are continuous and rapid,
I am forced to believe that college won't
go as well as planned,
How I long to continually feel avid,
The social pressure and aims to make friends
are the strongest demands.

I've been told that people at college are mature,
Supposedly, they're kind and they understand,
So, I hope this is true and they accept me more,
As in a lost, lonely, lame world I don't want to land.

Past relationships and previous experiences haven't
always been the best,
Despite the fact I've always tried hard to fit in,
At college, I just want to be able to rest,
I realise now, there's no competition; I don't need to win.

My main hope for the daunting prospect,
Is to be accepted, have fun and make friends,
College needs to be a place where I can be myself
and enjoy set projects,
I no longer want to have to pretend.

I can hear everyone saying that it will be okay,
But still I sit here frozen in fright and staring blankly,
The anxiety-provoking situation draws closer every day,
So I don't have much longer of this dread, fear and upset
thankfully.

Ghost

This poem represents how difficult it is to be seen and heard by others when you have a hidden disability. I wrote this poem when I was at college, to express that I felt constantly alone, particularly when in a group of people. Everyone else seemed to be accepted, but I struggled to be understood.

I sit in the canteen,
Surrounded by hustle and bustle,
A chaotic environment,
I sit in the corner alone – I am invisible.

I sit in the classroom,
Trying to focus, using up all of my energy to block out the rude comments and demoralising
language from my peers,
I've been told their behaviour is "normal banter,"
I am invisible.

I am the shy one,
The one who is recognised in the comfort of my home but disregarded in society,
It is like I'm a ghost – not being seen or heard,
I'm disguised by the shadows, fading to a blur.

My voice is quiet,
I continually repeat what I say,
In the hope that people will listen and understand,
I stand up for my rights – speak my valid opinion,
But still, I am invisible – I am a ghost.

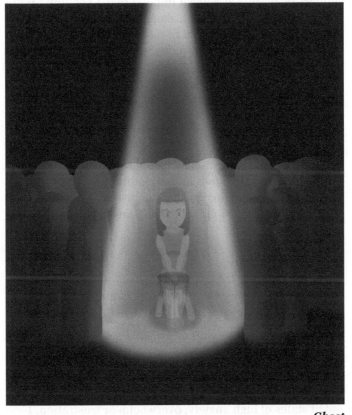

Ghost

I Have a Voice

A poem I've written whilst I was studying at college. As I can find verbal communication difficult, especially when I'm upset, frustrated or overwhelmed, I prefer to write down my thoughts to help express myself. Although, a specialist support instructor at college implied that I shouldn't write down my thoughts (through email) and, instead, I should openly talk about them face to face. At college, I was made to feel belittled and that my thoughts and feelings weren't valued. This poem aims to express the importance of listening to people on the autism spectrum and hearing what they would like and what support they need, rather than making assumptions.

Presumptions defining autistic people are incorrect,
The stigmatism surrounding the condition is demoralising,
We need to join together to bust the myths,
And show the true colours of the autism spectrum.

I have a voice,
Everyone has a voice,
We should all have the opportunity to communicate,
Communication is essential; a vital skill for survival in
the socially orientated society.

Just because I'm autistic,
It doesn't mean I am incapable of hearing what others say,
understanding language, decision making or expressing myself.
I can use words to tell you how I feel,
But at states of high anxiety, overwhelm or frustration, I
turn to poetry.

Please do not talk about me behind my back, for I can hear
the whispers you attempt to hide.
Please do not discuss my life with others before I give my
permission; I have the same rights as anyone else.

Please do not assume I don't understand what you say; my
strong intellect allows me to
comprehend more than you can imagine.
Please do not assume I am voiceless, because I'm autistic;
I may be painfully shy at times,
But my thoughts are loud and fierce.

When I talk, people are either shocked or just disregard my voice,
"Was that a whisper from the lonely corner I just heard?"
I can speak for myself and educate others – using my voice,
Before you make assumptions or judgments, you should
listen... listen to my voice.

Maybe if you listen,
You'll discover the depths of a mystical world,
You'll capture and embrace my emotions,
You'll learn something new about the wacky world we live in,
And I might just listen to you.

Hear... Listen... Understand,
The accumulation of our thoughts is probably greater than yours,
Trust me, if you listen to the autistic individual, you will learn.
We should stand to give a voice to the voiceless – we need
our voice to be heard...
You need to listen.

I have a voice

I Notice What You Don't Notice

This poem explores how I pay extra attention to detail; I often notice things that others don't. Through this poem I aim to portray how hard I try to conform on a daily basis; however, I feel that sometimes the neurotypical world should do more to accommodate the autistic mind. I am aware of my differences, but I am also aware of how society perceives these differences – often in a negative light.

I try so hard to notice when someone smiles at me,
I try so hard not to notice how loudly a door slams
when someone storms through.
I try so hard to notice when someone glances at
me to gain my attention,
I try so hard not to notice the dropping of a pen on a
wooden floor.
I try so hard to notice when boys wink at me –
are they just a friend or is it a flirtatious remark?
I try so hard not to notice when someone scrapes
something like nails on a blackboard.
I try so hard to notice when someone walks towards
me to start a conversation,
I try so hard not to notice the rude remarks from
people my age.
I try so hard to notice if someone says they want
to be my friend,
I try so hard not to notice the weird looks people give me.
I try so hard to notice when someone says "thank you" or
"I'm sorry" to cheer me up,
I try so hard not to notice the ghastly 'clean' smell of the
cutlery when it comes out of the dishwasher.

I try so hard, every day, just to be like you,
But why should I?
You need to appreciate that I am different from the crowd,
I may have weaknesses, but my strengths will get me far.
Treat me with respect and accept the way I am. That's all I ask.
Make whatever assumptions you like,
But, just remember, my life has always been a slow,
long, fearful hike.

Please Don't Give up on Me

A poem I've written to provide a personal contrast between society's perceptions of the positives and negatives of autism. Often, how people perceive me is the complete opposite to the truth.

I may seem quiet, but I can shout loud,
I may appear weak, but my mind is strong,
I may, at times, be unable to verbalise my thoughts,
but I am not voiceless,
I may become overwhelmed in everyday situations,
but I can raise awareness so that others understand,
I may be particularly anxious over simplistic matters,
but I take pleasure from the little things in life,
I may be frightened of social interactions,
but I have found strategies to help me cope,
I may not be very popular, but I do have a couple of good
friends who truly appreciate the complex wiring of my mind,
I may feel self-conscious, but I've been told I'm pretty and
have a loving heart,
I may be painfully shy, but once I get to know people
I might not stop talking,
I may be easily fixated by people or objects,
but I can use these to help mould my future,
I may experience intense emotions, but I can use
these to inspire others.

I may have a disability, but I have amazing abilities.

Please do not give up on me,
You may choose to disregard my feelings,
because I'm autistic,
You may think, because you're 'neurotypical',
you're worth more than me,
But, I have a powerful connection with the outer world;
one that you may never understand.

Please do not give up on me,
My feelings, thoughts and ideas can inspire the uninspired,
They can motivate the demotivated,
And they can educate the uneducated,
All I ask is for you to have faith in me and welcome my
mind into the very 'standard' society.

Meet Me Halfway

This poem is based on a judgemental comment that was made to me by a specialist support instructor at college. Insisting that I meet her halfway, especially when under tremendous pressure, led to me feeling disheartened and despondent.

You don't understand the depths of my emotion, when you push me into doing things I feel uncomfortable with. You don't truly understand the intensity of the anxiety I experience, so, don't say that I don't meet you halfway.

To walk down the street with bustling crowds and flashing lights, to sit in a class full of commotion and chaos, to sit in the canteen, desperate for friendship, a sense of belonging, causes me immense anxiety and makes me urge to escape.

At college, I have to mask my personality, battle my constant fears, and try to act up to any expectations you set, and you have the audacity to say I don't meet you halfway.

I might be lucky – I have all that I need. But when my anxiety and negative self-talk overflows, I crumble. Obviously I'm lucky – autism is a gift, a treasure, something to be proud of, but I struggle immensely with almost everything you take for granted.

Look at how far I've come, I've survived the shudders of secondary school, endured prom, and started college all on my own. Would you rather me make continual but gradual progress, or do you want me to fail and break down under pressure?

There's all or nothing in my world – it's called black and white thinking – struggling to read between the lines, I either do something I feel happy and content with or I do absolutely nothing at all.

So, when you push me into doing something: role plays, presentations, a work placement... I refuse and break down, simply because it's overwhelming; how do you expect me to cope?

I know you think you know how to help me; you work in the field of inclusive practice, but actually, you don't know me – I am an individual with autism. I am the only one who knows what's best, you don't know me – but I do! Don't try and put words into my mouth – trust me – it doesn't work!

My knowledge probably comes across as intimidating, I've researched the condition endlessly. I've devised a set of my own coping mechanisms, what works for one child with autism, probably won't work for me – recognising individuality is the key!

Socialising is draining – exhausting and overwhelming, To say hello to a friend is just as hard for me as starting a job is for you – daunting and frightening, I have less social energy than you to start with, So, imagine how tired I feel by the end of every day – Any additional stress and anxiety causes a shutdown – This causes an inability to function or communicate at all.

I may be socially inept, considered unsociable, But, sometimes your social skills can be just as poor, I don't think you realise how excruciatingly difficult it is for me to make friends at the best of times, It becomes near impossible to develop a friendship with added pressure.

The frustrations I experience continually, on a day to day basis, may seem unimportant to you – ridiculous maybe, You can block out the world whenever you want – I can't, I am constantly trapped in a world which seems isolating, confusing and demoralising – I feel deflated. Yet you feel you can make comments, like "you're not meeting me halfway."

Some may say I've been sheltered, protected from the world, I've felt secure for too long, well, I'm now in the outer world, being thrown into the deep end, and I've instantly realised one of the most important things.

I've said it before and will continue to say it until the message is clear, autism is a spectrum condition, not every person on the spectrum is the same! The fact is often missed as people with autism share certain traits, But, honestly, we all have different needs and one box doesn't help us at all – We don't want to be categorised into what you see as the 'norm' or 'correct way of society.'

I am a person with autism – I am human and I have feelings, I have a voice and a right to express my own valued opinions, so, next time you imply you want me to meet you halfway, question your knowledge beforehand and consider how making unfair, judgemental, detrimental comments will help me cope.

I will continue to fight for my rights – I've fought from the second I was born, I believe I should be respected and my differences embraced, my needs challenged but at my own pace, my positive contributions and achievements should be acknowledged for one and celebrated for another.

I think you should start listening to my voice, quiet but fierce, and meet me halfway! Don't discriminate or stereotype – just accept and support me, in the suggested ways!

Autism awareness is a highlight for me, no matter how many books you've read, videos you've watched or people you've spoken to about the subject, if you haven't walked my long trudge of a path, you don't have a true understanding of the disability.

That's right – I have a disability, a hidden disability, where guilt, shame, upset, anger and anxiety threaten to trickle through when I'm overwhelmed, my life is a battle – a rollercoaster – a challenge, so, maybe you should, for once, meet me halfway!

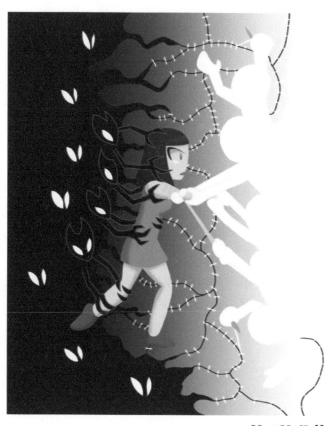

Meet Me Halfway

Think of the Consequences

After expressing my anxieties and frustrations about the chaotic, disruptive and unsupportive classroom environment at college, I was told by a specialist support instructor I needed to 'think of the consequences.'

I tried my hardest to raise awareness and
understanding of autism throughout the college,
I tried my hardest to endure the lack of understanding
from 'specialist' support staff
and a lack of knowledge from my peers,
I tried my hardest to ignore patronising comments,
and battle through, pretending I was in another
planet, as it was said that everyone else was 'normal.'

The disrespectful, disgusting and demoralising
language from my classmates was
considered to be 'normal banter',
The fundraising and awareness projects I organised
weren't acknowledged or praised,
I was told I needed support to get distinctions
in my assignments,
despite my unnoticed high level of intellect,
Yet, when I stood up for my rights, I was told to
think of the consequences.

I vented my ongoing frustrations in the only
way I knew how,
I made myself loud and clear,
I stood up to support others in surviving the
bustling college environment,
And I managed to communicate my complex,
confused and anxious thoughts,
but, all you can say is that I didn't think of the
consequences.

I know you think you supported me through college
by providing emotional support on how my behaviour
can affect others,
But, actually, you didn't know me well enough
to realise I am a very respectful, intelligent and
determined individual
who doesn't need to be patronised into a corner.
I find, there are very few people who have a genuine
understanding of autism,
and it takes inspiration, determination and passion
from autistic individuals
for neuro-typicals to realise the true extent of the
challenges we face on a daily basis.

Have you ever thought of the consequences when you
made patronising comments to me?
Did you ever think of the consequences when you
pushed me into doing things
I was uncomfortable with and say you helped,
when it was my motivation, determination, willpower
and support from friends that got me through?
Have you ever thought of the consequences
when you allowed others to take credit for everything
I arranged at college?
Did you ever think of the consequences
when you put the 'inclusive practice' qualification in
front of the calming, considerate, enthusiastic, caring,
encouraging and understanding approach you need to
have when working with autistic individuals?

Teenagers

This poem is based on society's perception of a neurotypical adolescent (a teenager who is not on the autism spectrum). This poem reflects upon preconceived ideas and stereotypes, which are not necessarily representative of all the young community. Therefore, it aims to portray the importance of getting to know people before making judgements.

Adolescence, a difficult time,
Teenagers the lemons, parents the lime.
Battling for independence,
Decreasing their attendance.

Friends are hard to find,
When the stresses are trying to unwind.
Keeping friends is another story,
But five years on, oh its glory.

Drugs, booze and smoke,
Always chatting up the nearest bloke.
Sex on their minds,
Pornography of all kinds.

Room is messy,
Until you see Grandma Betty.
Posters of celebs and crushes,
It's surprising how quick the blood rushes.

Teenagers are misunderstood,
Shy ones hiding under their hood.
Some are confident, vivacious and daring,
Others are introverted, self-conscious and over-caring.

Christmas Time

A poem I've written to highlight some of the anxieties that people with autism may have about the festive season. Christmas is an exciting time for many but can create overwhelming sensations for those with autism.

A time full of commotion, crowds and cheer,
Strange men dressed as Santa, gathered in
pubs slurping pints of beer,
Fill some autistic people with confusion and fear,
Their comfort zones float away – nowhere near.

Funny looking, coloured trees and sparkly decorations,
A confusing, unusual, anxiety-provoking creation,
People with autism could be fascinated by the
decorative tessellations,
Using their special interests can help them free their aggravations.

Distant relatives appear out of the blue,
And they expect individuals with autism to have
learnt all of the social cues,
The relatives come all that way to invade privacy
and have a brew,
Said they've missed you and have thought of you
all year... how is this true?

Hitting the stores is another stressful matter,
Can't hear yourself think amongst all the chatter,
Crowds barge past, their painful touches triggering a
meltdown, but was supposed to be a way to flatter,
Too many things to look at, sparkly decorations,
flashing lights and disgusting food platters,
Causing a sensory overload – overwhelming,
daunting, frustrating – people with autism turn to batter.

Parties, pantomimes and festive meals,

The social fake is exhausting, as tough as fruit peel,
The fatigue caused through social interaction is difficult
to express and reveal,
That's why everyone in the community should light it up teal.

Christmas dinners are hard to eat,
Some autistics dislike the textures of meat,
The parent's encouraging battle continues –
the person with autism will not be defeated,
The mashed foods have to be arranged on the
'clean smelling' plate neatly.

Christmas is supposed to be a time full of fun,
laughter and joy,
But to some people on the autistic spectrum,
all the festive season does is annoy,
Please, accept and try to understand autism,
not only apparent in boys,
As maybe then, the anxiety, stress and fear could be
reduced and people with autism may appreciate the toys.

University

This poem is based on one of my friends who is also on the autism spectrum. I wrote this poem for her when she was preparing for university studies. Considering college lecturers believed she wouldn't be capable of attending university, I am extremely proud that she is now in her second year. It is my dream to undertake a BA Honours in Special Education and an MA in Autism – and no-one will stop me!

I want you to be successful,
My dream is for you to be happy,
I want you to accomplish your dreams,
I hope that you continue to enjoy life.

But, I don't want you to leave,
I know you'll be back, but you won't be at The Bay,
It will be so different without you,
Not as fun, enthusiastic or inspiring.

I'll really miss you,
Please keep in touch,
We'll definitely remain friends,
And connect in whatever way we can.

Good luck for university,
I hope you thrive, have fun and spread positivity continually,
I hope you make good friends,
And if you do ever get stressed or anxious,
remember I'll always be here for you.

I hope you achieve your dreams,
Inspire and motivate others in the team,
Work towards all of your goals,
And never fall into a dark and gloomy hole.
You've taught me that I no longer have to pretend,
Because of you, I now have a best friend.

Life

This poem provides an inspirational message of positivity. Sending happy vibes throughout, this poem aims to encourage everyone to make the most out of life and feel comfortable being themselves.

Life is short,
Make people proud,
And smile with the crowd.

Life is short,
Laugh every day,
For then the memories you can relay.

Life is short,
Never judge others,
As sometimes the sad smiles are the protective covers.

Life is short,
Never underestimate yourself,
Accept your wonderful self.

Life is short,
Always try your best,
And just forget the rest.

Life is short,
Love others unconditionally,
Express yourself passionately.

Life is short,
Cry loudly to show your emotion,
And to also express your devotion.

Life is short,
Never forget those you love,
But, don't let them stop you from looking above.

Life is short,
Dream big and accept a challenge,
Take small steps that you can manage.

Life is short,
Enjoy everything you do,
Don't waste time feeling blue,
For there's only ever going to be one person like you!

<u>Contact</u>

I hope that you've all enjoyed reading through the variety of poetry on offer. I hope that my poetry has captivated your emotions and given you a clearer insight into what life is like living with autism.

Please contact me via 'A Different Perspective' on Facebook and Twitter.

www.adifferentperspective.info